BEING ADOPTED

BEING ADOPTED

by **MAXINE B. ROSENBERG**

photographs by
GEORGE ANCONA

Lothrop, Lee & Shepard Books   New York

Text copyright © 1984 by Maxine B. Rosenberg. Photographs copyright © 1984 by
George Ancona. All rights reserved. No part of this book may be reproduced or
utilized in any form or by any means, electronic or mechanical, including
photocopying, recording or by any information storage and retrieval system, without
permission in writing from the Publisher. Inquiries should be addressed to Lothrop,
Lee & Shepard Books, a division of William Morrow & Company, Inc., 1350 Avenue
of the Americas, New York, New York 10019. Printed in the United States of America.
First Edition.   8   9   10   11   12   13   14   15   16   17

LIBRARY OF CONGRESS CATALOGING IN PUBLICATION DATA
Rosenberg, Maxine B.   Being adopted.   Summary: Several young children recount
their experiences as adopted members of their families.   1. Adoption—Juvenile
literature.   2. Adoptees—Family relationships—Juvenile literature.   [1. Adoption]
I. Ancona, George, ill.   II. Title.   HV873.R67   1984   362.7′34   83-17522
ISBN 0-688-02672-9   ISBN 0-688-02673-7 (lib. bdg.)

To Karin, Seth, David, and Mark—
who are delightful
M.B.R.

To Helena and Modesto Carvalhosa
G.A.

When Rebecca was five, she said there are two ways babies are born: One is coming out of a mother's body, and the other is coming from an airplane.

Rebecca believed this because an airplane brought her to her mom and dad. When she was eight weeks old, she flew halfway across the United States to become her parents' third child. Rebecca is adopted.

Now that she is seven, Rebecca knows all babies come from a mother's body. Like many adopted children, however, she does not remember her birth mother.

Ten-year-old Andrei and eight-year-old Karin are also adopted. Andrei came from India to become his parents' first child.

Karin, from Korea, became her parents' fourth.

But no matter what country adopted children come from or who their birth parents were, they are as much a part of their families as any brothers or sisters born to their adoptive parents. The only difference is that adopted children arrive in another way.

In the beginning, adopted children often feel frightened. So much around them is different, including their new families.

"I screamed and kicked when Mommy and Daddy hugged me," says Andrei, remembering when he was four and a half and first met his adoptive parents. "I didn't know who they were. 'Take me back to my friends in India,' I yelled in Hindi. But nobody understood me.

"Then later, when I saw my photograph in the house, and my parents told me in sign language that their home was my home too, I was so happy I ran wild through the rooms!"

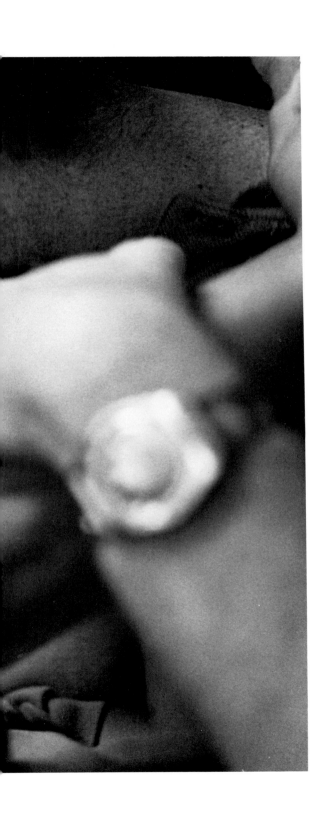

"I was a baby when I came to my family," says Karin, "but Mommy tells me I still was frightened. Whenever she or Daddy cuddled me, I'd grab my hair and pull out large clumps. And if the telephone rang, I jumped. But in a few months I calmed down and now I love being held."

It usually takes about six months for parents and children to get to know one another whether the children are adopted or not. With older adopted children, as with Andrei, it may take longer.

After a while, though, everyone learns how much they need and care about each other, even for little things.

Without Rebecca's help, for example, no one can get the cat to leave the tree. But when Rebecca meows, he jumps into her arms.

And Karin knows she can rely on her mom or dad to come to

he rescue whenever monsters sneak into her room at night.

It feels good to be part of a family and to be wanted. Yet there are times when adopted children wish they had another mom or dad. Often, just like most children, they feel this way after they've been scolded.

So they may dream about living with their birth mother
or father, even if they don't really remember that parent at
all. They may pretend to go hunting for tigers in the
jungles of India or dress up in satin robes like kings or
queens. Whatever they make believe, it never includes a
mom or dad who yells or gets cross.

Usually these dreams about their birth parents happen less often over time. After one or two years with their adoptive families, most adopted children would agree with Karin, who says, "I'm glad I'm adopted. I like my mom and dad, and I love my dog."

Once in a while, someone—a stranger perhaps
—may wonder out loud why an adopted child

looks different from other members in his or her family.

Even good friends may be curious.

"How come you don't look like your mom?" Rebecca was asked more than once.

"Because I'm adopted," she replied. Rebecca, like many adopted children, didn't like to be reminded that she stood out. It hurt even more when people also asked why her birth mother didn't keep her.

That's something Rebecca, Andrei, and Karin have thought about a lot. They have asked their moms and dads, too, about how their adoption happened, where they were born, and what their birth parents looked like. Was there anything special about their birth parents that might have been passed along to them? Were there other children in the family? It's confusing, they say, having two mothers, two families. And sometimes they even worry that adoption was their fault—that they did something wrong, like cry too much, to make their birth families give them up. Karin, for example, used to think her birth parents gave her up because she had so much hair and was ugly.

Like most adoptive parents, Rebecca's, Andrei's, and Karin's could not answer all these questions, but they told them everything they knew.

"Your father was black, like your daddy," Rebecca's mom said. "And your mother was part white and part Cheyenne Indian. Both were tall, like you, and healthy and young."

Rebecca's mom didn't know why Rebecca's birth parents had chosen adoption. Maybe they were too young, she suggested. It's hard to take care of a baby when you're young, *any* baby. Some young parents feel adoption is the best way to make sure their child can have a good home.

Karin's and Andrei's parents also didn't know why their children's birth parents had chosen adoption. Since their birth countries, Korea and India, have many poor people, they said, their birth families may have felt adoption would give Karin and Andrei a better life.

"Or maybe my mother died," says Andrei. That could, in fact, be true.

However different their birth families may be, Karin, Andrei, and Rebecca have one thing in common: The reason they were given up for adoption was not their fault. Almost all parents want to keep their children. Choosing adoption is usually a very hard decision. Karin's, Andrei's, and Rebecca's parents say that what's most important is that the children now have a family that will care for them always.

Still, Rebecca is sometimes uneasy. She would prefer to have been born from the same mother as Greg and Leslie, her brother and sister. "Then I wouldn't worry at night about Mommy and Daddy giving me up," she says.

"Mommy and Daddy can't get rid of you," Greg tells her. "I was there when they signed papers saying you're in this family *forever.*"

"So that means we three have to stick together," adds Leslie.

It has taken time, too, for Karin to be happy with the way she looks. Just as Dara, the tallest girl in her class, wishes she were smaller, Karin would like to look like nearly everyone else.

"I hate when people ask if I'm Chinese," Karin says. "Since I couldn't make my eyes round, one day I tried to change my hair by wearing my grandma's wig."

"Silly, blondes get freckles," her friend Alicia reminded her, "while we Koreans tan so nicely." Alicia is adopted too.

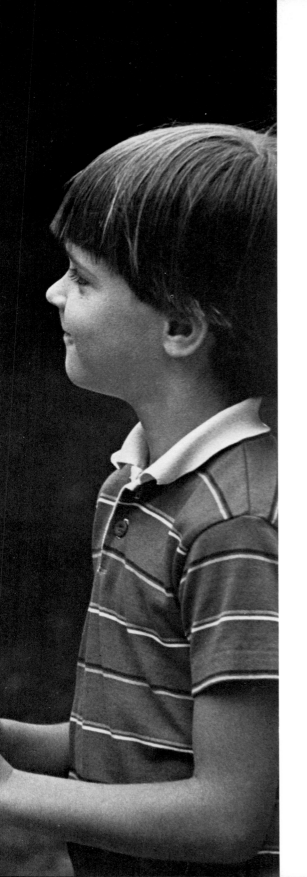

And, although he knew his family cared for him, Andrei found it difficult coming from a different country. He wanted to look like most Americans he saw. When he first arrived in this country, he wouldn't talk to anyone from India, and he even drew himself blue-eyed and fair. Looking at the picture with his friend Brendan, he said, "Now we're both vanilla."

At home, though, Andrei liked hearing stories about the Punjab, the state where he was born, and baking chapatti, Indian wheat bread, with his dad. Best of all, he loved eating in Indian restaurants.

Then last year, in third grade, his class learned about India in Social Studies.

"I wore an Indian wedding outfit and a turban to school," he remembers proudly.

Now Andrei is an American.
So is Karin. They became
citizens after living in the United
States for two years. "But India is
my country too," Andrei says.
"One day I'm going back to visit
my hometown."

Meanwhile he keeps busy
playing soccer with his eight-
year-old brother, Nicholas.
Nicholas, also from India, was
adopted ten months ago.

"I wish my parents would adopt another child," says Karin, "a sister I could boss around." Karin's mom has said that four children are plenty in their house. Instead, Karin's mother has told other parents about children who are waiting to be adopted.

"Adoption is a good idea," Rebecca now says. "It gives children a home if they don't have any. Maybe I'll adopt when I'm older. Except it has to be a girl. With curly hair and black eyes. And she'll be brown. Just like me."

ABOUT ADOPTION TODAY

With the American family in transition, it is no wonder that considerable changes have also taken place in adoption. Most noticeable in recent years is the increase in transracial and transcultural adoptions, usually white parents adopting foreign-born or minority American children. Sociologists cite two primary factors contributing to this trend, factors that are likely to continue: the unavailability of healthy white infants as more white unwed mothers keep their babies; and a new type of adoptive parent—single or married, with or without biological children—who adopts for religious, social, or humanitarian reasons.

Experts have found that there are various stages in any adoptive child's adjustment. In the early years (ages 3-6), for example, when the child asks about birth and learns about his biological parents, he tends to focus on his relationship with his mother. "Why couldn't the lady who had me keep me?" "Who is my real mother?" and "How can I have two mothers?" are common questions asked. Then as the child moves on to the middle years (ages 6-11), she may blame herself for being given up and, subconsciously, fear that it may happen again.

With transracial and transcultural adoption, there are additional problems. These children often not only look different from their neighbors, schoolmates, and friends, but they stand out in their own families as well. And adopted children, like most children, want to fit in. Initially, to compensate for their differences in appearance and nationality, minority adopted children may go overboard to "be American." Parents, though, who encourage pride in their child's heritage, can help the child strike a healthy balance.

Also, because foreign-born children generally arrive in this country with little background information, it is difficult for them to find answers to the inevitable questions about their roots. Parents need to answer these questions honestly and as best they can, within the framework of the child's understanding. And, as for each stage in the adopted child's adjustment, they need to reassure the child how much they love and want him, emphasizing that love is not bound by physical appearance. A child should feel she is special, apart from whatever qualities she has inherited.